ELECTRICITY IN ACTION

POWER TRIP!
THE FUTURE OF ELECTRICITY

by Jenny Mason

CAPSTONE PRESS
a capstone imprint

Published by Capstone Press, an imprint of Capstone
1710 Roe Crest Drive, North Mankato, Minnesota 56003
capstonepub.com

Copyright © 2026 by Capstone. All rights reserved. No part of this publication may be reproduced in whole or in part, or stored in a retrieval system, or transmitted in any form or by any means, electronic, mechanical, photocopying, recording, or otherwise, without written permission of the publisher.

Library of Congress Cataloging-in-Publication Data is available on the Library of Congress website.

ISBN: 9798875222306 (hardcover)
ISBN: 9798875222252 (paperback)
ISBN: 9798875222269 (ebook PDF)

Summary: Scientists and engineers are developing environmentally friendly ways to generate power. Discover the new technologies that harness electricity from sunlight, wind, water, and more.

Editorial Credits
Editor: Ashley Kuehl; Designer: Sarah Bennett; Media Researcher: Rebekah Hubstenberger ; Production Specialist: Tori Abraham

Image Credits
Alamy: Westend61 GmbH, 12; Getty Images: Alistair Berg, 26, Dan Goshtigian/The Boston Globe, 8, FADEL SENNA/AFP, 9, Farouk Batiche/Anadolu Agency, 10, Fei Yang, 15, Grant Faint, 19, iStock/elenabs, 22, iStock/MonumentalDoom, 16, iStock/VectorMine, 6, Janos Kummer, 18, Lin Shanchuan/Xinhua News Agency, 13, MARK GARLICK/SCIENCE PHOTO LIBRARY, 29, PATRICK KOVARIK/AFP, 27, prognone, 7, Rafael Dols, 25, Rapeepong Puttakumwong, 28, RUNSTUDIO, 4, Scott Heins, 21; Shutterstock: Daniel Soutinho, 14, I. Rottlaender, 23, Kletr, 24, Olha1981, 17, pan denim, cover, thelamephotographer, 11

Design Elements
Shutterstock: galihprihatama, Iurii Motov

Any additional websites and resources referenced in this book are not maintained, authorized, or sponsored by Capstone. All product and company names are trademarks™ or registered® trademarks of their respective holders.

Printed and bound in China. 006276

Table of Contents

INTRODUCTION
WIRED...................................4

CHAPTER 1
HARVEST THE SKIES......................6

CHAPTER 2
FLOWING WATER AND SHATTERING ATOMS....14

CHAPTER 3
GRIDLOCKED............................20

CHAPTER 4
THE POWER OF ZERO WASTE..............24

GLOSSARY.......................30
READ MORE......................31
INTERNET SITES.................31
INDEX..........................32
ABOUT THE AUTHOR...............32

Words in **bold** are in the glossary.

INTRODUCTION
WIRED

Plug in. Flip a switch. Power stations deliver instant electricity. It travels through cables across the country. But most power plants burn polluting **fossil fuels**. Luckily, we have cleaner ways to generate power. We have sunlight, wind, and water. We have mirrors, salt, rubber bands, and even juice!

WHAT'S THE BUZZ ON ELECTRICITY?

What is electricity?
Electricity is a natural force. It can be used to make light and heat or to make machines work.

Where does electricity come from?
Everything in the universe is made of super-tiny building blocks called **atoms**. Each atom has **protons**, **neutrons**, and **electrons**. Sometimes, electrons can move from one atom to the next. That movement creates electricity.

What's the difference between a conductor and an insulator?
Electricity moves through **conductors**. Conductors are materials that help electrons flow easily. Water and certain metals are conductors. **Insulators** slow or stop the flow of electrons. Wood, plastic, and rubber are insulators.

How is electricity measured?
Amps tell you how quickly the electrons are moving. Volts tell you how much pressure there is on the electrons. The energy of electricity can be put to work. The difficulty of the work is measured in watts.

Watts = Amps x Volts

CHAPTER 1
HARVEST THE SKIES

Solar energy systems turn sunlight into electricity. All light is made of **photons**. Photovoltaic (PV) cells are super thin chips with special minerals. Photons crash into the minerals. That pushes electrons into motion. This electrical current flows to power stations that supply towns and cities.

PV cells stack up thin layers of minerals, plastic, and glass. Photons crash into electrons in the minerals. This crash knocks the electrons loose from their protons. Flowing electrons create electrical currents. The glass and plastic protect the minerals from damage.

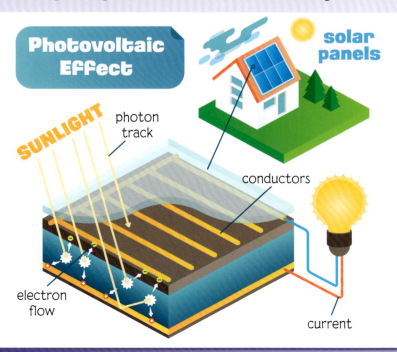

Mirror, Mirror on the Wall

Concentrating Solar Power (CSP) systems use mirrors and photons. They focus the sun's beams onto a receiver. Receivers are tubes of oils or salt that heat up fast. Power stations use the heat to make electricity. Heat can also be stored for later.

This CSP system collects solar energy. One CSP plant can generate enough energy to power 90,000 homes.

Maria Telkes invented the first solar-powered home heating system in the 1940s. She was nicknamed the Sun Queen.

Positives and Negatives

Solar power is **renewable** energy. It never runs out. Solar is quiet. It does not pollute the air. But this bright energy has a dark side. The minerals in PV cells must be mined. Mining can cause air and water pollution. As trash in landfills, old solar panels release **toxins**.

Sun Paint and Night Sponges

Scientists are developing super tiny solar cells. They are small enough to sit on a soap bubble. But they can produce a lot of power. These tiny cells could be painted on buildings. Imagine wall paint powering the lights!

New PV cells can work at night. They act like sponges. They soak up leftover heat from the sun.

As of 2025, the world's largest concentrated solar plant was in Morocco. The plant is the size of 3,500 football fields.

No Gust, No Glory

Wind is also renewable energy. Ancient windmills pumped water. Modern wind turbines have long, slender blades. The blades spin a shaft that turns magnets. Electrons in the wire wrapped around the magnets flow through cables as electricity.

Many old turbine blades end up in landfills. A few are recycled, such as the ones in this playground in the Netherlands.

A semi truck carries a wind turbine blade along a highway.

FACT

On most wind turbines, each blade can be from about 165 to over 350 feet (50 to 107 meters) long.

Eagles vs. Turbines

Each year, wind turbines kill about one million birds. Eagles are especially at risk. They fly so fast that the white blades look like a faint blur. Scientists have started painting one blade black. Eagles spot that blade. They dodge the turbine!

A wind turbine with a black blade is easier for birds to see.

Never Stop

High in Earth's atmosphere, wind never stops blowing. Special kites could harvest this energy. At bladeless wind stations on Earth, wind jiggles rubber bands and towers. The jiggling moves electrons in the air. Wide fins, or air scoops, on rooftops could capture wind energy.

Workers install a turbine as part of an offshore wind farm near southeast China.

FACT

In 2023, China started building the world's largest offshore wind turbine. Its blades will be 460 feet (140 m) long!

13

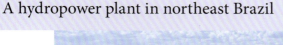
FLOWING WATER AND SHATTERING ATOMS

Flowing water can also generate electricity. **Hydropower** has been used since 1882. It is the oldest renewable energy in the United States. River dams form lakes called **reservoirs**. When water flows through the dam, it spins turbine generators. Dams do not burn fossil fuels. But they do flood animal habitats.

A hydropower plant in northeast Brazil

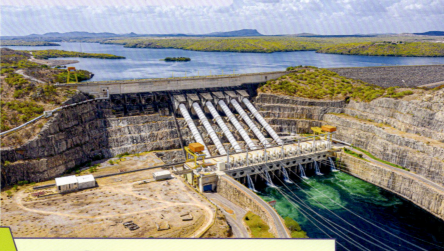

FACT
Hydropower creates about one-half to three-quarters of Brazil's electricity.

Pump It Up

Pumped storage systems may be the future of hydropower. Engineers create two lakes. One is on higher ground. Water pours downhill to the lower one. The water flows through turbines and creates electricity. Pumps recycle the water back to the upper lake. These systems do not harm river ecosystems.

A pumped storage system in China

Deep Sea Batteries

Did you know natural battery nuggets pepper the ocean floor? They are made of tiny metal particles. The particles have clumped together over millions of years. These metals are used in electric car batteries. Some companies want to harvest these nuggets. But the process would kill millions of sea animals and plants!

A nugget made of metal particles, taken from the ocean floor

FACT

Robots sent to harvest nuggets could destroy octopus nurseries. Those are places where octopuses lay eggs.

Surf's Up

Researchers want to harness ocean waves for electricity. The ocean is always in motion. And water pushes harder than air. Many devices are being tested. The best design must survive salt water and crushing sea storms. It must also keep ocean creatures safe.

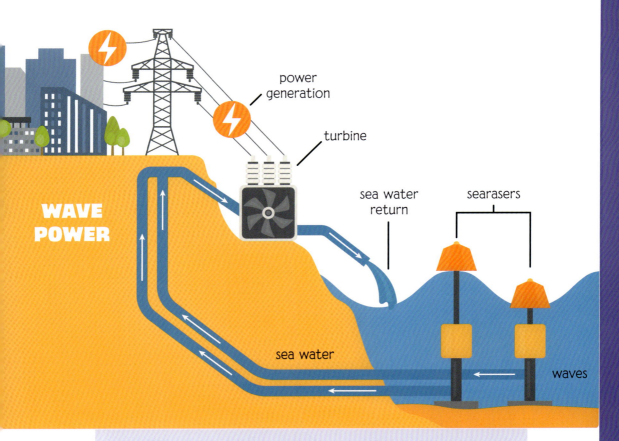

This diagram shows one of many possible designs for wave power systems. Waves lift and lower searasers, which act as pumps, driving water through pipes to a turbine generator.

A nuclear power plant in Mochovce, Slovakia

Atom Cracking

Nuclear power plants produce electricity by cracking atoms apart. Breaking them releases intense heat. Most nuclear plants use the mineral **uranium**. But mining for uranium is destructive. And it becomes very toxic when used for nuclear power. After it's been used, the mineral must be stored away for 1 million years!

Full Steam Ahead

In Earth's core, atoms sloshing in a hot mineral soup shatter constantly. This produces **geothermal** heat. That heat can turn turbines. Or it can heat homes or bathwater. It replaces electric or water heaters. Nine out of 10 homes in Iceland are heated with geothermal power.

A geothermal station in Iceland

FACT

Geo means earth. *Thermal* means heat. The geothermal core can get as hot as the sun's surface. That's about 10,800 degrees Fahrenheit (6,000 degrees Celsius)!

CHAPTER 3
GRIDLOCKED

Every time you plug in a device, you rev up the power grid. The grid is made up of power plants across the U.S. and Canada. Fuel-burning plants, wind, solar, and hydropower all contribute. Millions of miles of cables connect power stations to towns and cities. The grid runs nonstop.

The Electric Orchestra

Thousands of people operate the grid. All of its generators are **synchronized**. But the grid is not perfect. One snapped cable means lights go out for thousands of people. Sometimes, too many buildings demand power at once. That overloads power stations. Generators shut down.

FACT

Thomas Edison designed the first power grid in New York in 1882. It sent power to 59 customers.

A 2019 power outage in New York City

Grid and Bear It

Humans' need for power continues to grow. What we call the power grid is actually made up of lots of tiny grids, or networks of energy. The networks connect to form the larger grid. In the future, each network will use many renewable sources. They could share extra power.

A model of how the electric grid might look in the future

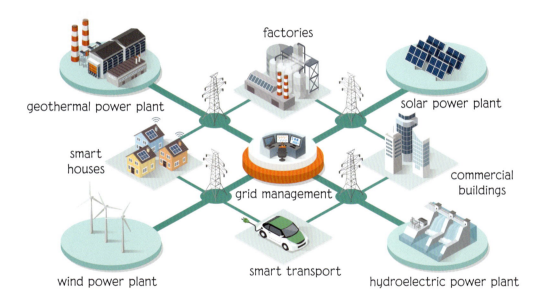

AC/DC

Electrons flowing together create electric current. In a direct current (DC), electrons flow in one steady direction. In an alternating current (AC), they are tugged back and forth. Power stations use AC. Its powerful energy waves zap across long distances. Batteries generate DC.

Make an Electron Race Track

Create your own DC circuit. It's like a race track for electrons.

Supplies:
- a graphite art pencil
- a sheet of paper
- tape
- a light-emitting diode (LED)
- a 9-volt battery

Steps:

1. Draw half an oval on the paper. Make a thick, solid line, but don't smear it. Draw the oval's other half, but leave a gap between the halves.

2. Label one side with a positive (+) mark. Label the other side with a negative (-) mark.

3. Bend the legs of the LED. Put it over one gap in the oval. Tape the longer leg to the positive line. Tape the shorter leg to the negative line.

4. Touch the terminals of the 9-volt battery to the other gap. Be sure the positive terminal touches the positive line. The negative terminal must touch the negative line.

5. What happens? If nothing, then try pressing the legs to the paper. The LED lights up!

6. What happens if you draw a longer race track? Or if you draw lighter or darker lines? How do you explain the new results?

CHAPTER 4
THE POWER OF ZERO WASTE

Power experts recommend we let nothing go to waste. Body waste usually goes down the toilet. But human and animal waste can generate electricity. These biofuels can be burned to make steam in power plants. When solid waste rots, it emits gases. These gases can be burned to make power.

This power plant in the Czech Republic turns waste from a pig farm into electricity.

Juiced by Juice

Did you know fruit and vegetable juice can make a solar panel? Plants contain chlorophyll, a material that absorbs light. Plant waste is blended into juice. The juice is poured over a flat surface. When it hardens, it creates a window pane that acts like a solar panel. Future skyscrapers could be solar farms.

FACT
One juice window can charge two phones per day.

The chlorophyll in plants uses sunlight as energy for food.

Power Plays

Tag! You're it! When you run, your movement is a form of energy. Some of that energy passes through your feet to the ground. Power tiles can absorb this energy. They can change it to electricity. Sports fields, dance clubs, and sidewalks could become power stations.

Fashion Trends

What if your clothes could charge a phone? Threads made of special minerals hold an electric charge. These threads are woven into clothes. When the fabric moves, stretches, or heats up, it charges the fibers. This charge can pass through the air to a phone battery or other device.

A coat with solar panels is modeled at a fashion show. The power collected from the panels can charge a mobile phone.

27

Slay Electricity Vampires

Electricity vampires in your home suck energy from wall outlets even when they are off. In the U.S., that burns about 48.5 million tons (44 million metric tons) of fossil fuels. With an adult's help, go on a vampire hunt. Slay these monsters by unplugging them.

Look for the following:
- toasters
- TVs
- laptop and phone chargers
- lamps
- fans
- video game consoles

Power Surge

Looking forward, humankind's power needs will surge. We can replace old fossil fuel technologies with cleaner inventions. But that requires making, storing, and moving more electricity. We must be creative while avoiding waste. That will help us solve the world's power supply problems.

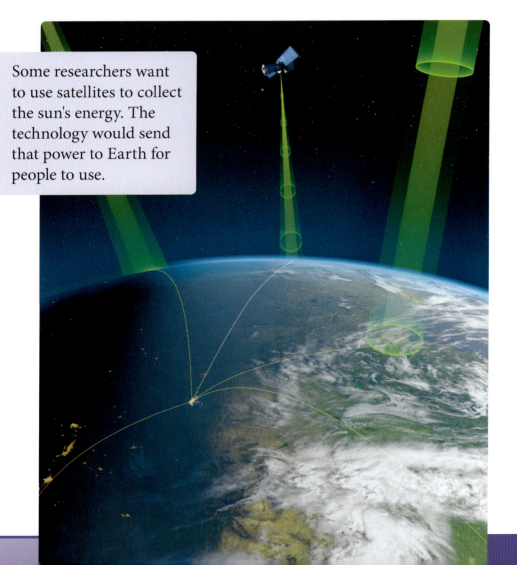

Some researchers want to use satellites to collect the sun's energy. The technology would send that power to Earth for people to use.

GLOSSARY

atom (AT-uhm)—an element in its smallest form

conductor (kuhn-DUHK-tuhr)—a material that lets electricity travel easily through it

electron (i-LEK-tron)—a negatively charged particle in an atom

fossil fuel (FAH-suhl FYOO-uhl)—coal, oil, or natural gas, formed from the remains of prehistoric plants and animals

geothermal (jee-oh-THUR-muhl)—heat inside Earth

hydropower (HYE-droh-pou-ur)—electricity made with water

insulator (IN-suh-late-ur)—a material that keeps electricity inside wires or paths

neutron (NOO-trahn)—a particle in the nucleus of an atom that has no electric charge

photon (FOH-tahn)—a tiny particle of light energy

proton (PRO-tahn)—positively charged particle in an atom

renewable (ri-NOO-uh-buhl)—resources that can't be used up

reservoir (REZ-ur-vwahr)—a lake in which water is stored for use

synchronized (SING-kruh-nizd)—set to the same time or order

toxin (TAHK-sin)—poison

uranium (yu-RAY-nee-uhm)—a radioactive material

READ MORE

Peterson, Megan Cooley. *Benjamin Franklin and the Discovery of Electricity: Separating Fact from Fiction*. Mankato, MN: Capstone Press, an imprint of Capstone, 2023.

Thatcher, Meg. *Using Solar Farms to Fight Climate Change*. Mendota Heights, MN: North Star Editions, 2023.

Twamley, Erin and Joshua Sneideman. *Renewable Energy: Power the World with Sustainable Fuel, with Hands-On Science Activities for Kids*. Norwich, VT: Nomad Press, 2024.

INTERNET SITES

Energy Kids U.S. Energy Information Administration
eia.gov/kids/

NASA Climate Kids
climatekids.nasa.gov/menu/energy/

Universe and More: Crack the Circuit
universeandmore.com/crack-the-circuit/

INDEX

atoms, 5, 18, 19

batteries, 16, 22, 23, 27
biofuels, 24

conductors, 5

dams, 14

eagles, 12
Edison, Thomas, 20
electrons, 5, 6, 10, 13, 22, 23

fossil fuels, 4, 14, 20, 28, 29

generators, 14, 17, 20
geothermal power, 19, 22

hydropower, 4, 14, 15, 17, 20, 22

neutrons, 5
nuclear power, 18

photons, 6, 7
pollution, 8
power grid, 20, 22
power plants, 4, 9, 18, 20, 22, 24

power stations, 4, 6, 7, 20, 22, 26

protons, 5, 6
PV cells, 6, 8, 9

solar power, 4, 6, 7, 8, 9, 20, 22, 25, 27, 29

turbines, 10, 11, 12, 13, 14, 15, 17, 19

uranium, 18

wind power, 4, 10, 11, 12, 13, 20, 22

ABOUT THE AUTHOR

Jenny Mason is a story-hunter. She explores foreign countries, canyon mazes, and burial crypts to gather the facts that make the best true tales. She'll interview NASA engineers or sniff a 200-year-old skull. Her research knows no bounds! Jenny received her MFA in Writing for Children and Young Adults from the Vermont College of Fine Arts. She also holds a Master of Philosophy from Trinity College Dublin. Find all of Jenny's books and projects at jynnemason.com.